HILLARY CLINTON
An American Journey

GROSSET & DUNLAP
Published by the Penguin Group
Penguin Group (USA) Inc., 375 Hudson Street,
New York, New York 10014, USA
Penguin Group (Canada), 90 Eglinton Avenue East, Suite 700,
Toronto, Ontario M4P 2Y3, Canada
(a division of Pearson Penguin Canada Inc.)
Penguin Books Ltd., 80 Strand, London WC2R 0RL, England
Penguin Group Ireland, 25 St. Stephen's Green, Dublin 2, Ireland
(a division of Penguin Books Ltd.)
Penguin Group (Australia), 250 Camberwell Road, Camberwell,
Victoria 3124, Australia
(a division of Pearson Australia Group Pty. Ltd.)
Penguin Books India Pvt. Ltd., 11 Community Centre, Panchsheel
Park, New Delhi—110 017, India
Penguin Group (NZ), 67 Apollo Drive, Rosedale, North Shore 0745,
Auckland, New Zealand
(a division of Pearson New Zealand Ltd.)
Penguin Books (South Africa) (Pty.) Ltd., 24 Sturdee Avenue,
Rosebank, Johannesburg 2196, South Africa

Penguin Books Ltd., Registered Offices: 80 Strand, London
WC2R 0RL, England

Photo Credits: Cover: © Associated Press; Title page: © Associated Press; Interior photos: page 4: Associated
Press; page 5: © Jacques M. Chenet/Liaison; pages 6-7: © Associated Press; page 16: © Hawes Alan/Corbis
Sygma; page 17: © Steve Liss/Getty Images; pages 18-19: © Brooks Kraft/Corbis; page 21: © Brooks Kraft
/Corbis; page 22: © Brooks Kraft/Corbis; page 23: © Corbis Sygma; page 24: © Associated Press; page 25:
© Wally McNamee/Corbis; page 27: © Stewart Mike/Corbis Sygma; page 28: © Associated Press; page 29:
© Associated Press; page 30: © Stewart Mike/Corbis Sygma; page 31: © Stewart Mike/Corbis Sygma; page 32:
© Associated Press; page 33: © Associated Press; page 34: © Reuters/Corbis; page 35: © Associated Press; page
39: © Associated Press; page 40: © Reuters/Corbis; page 41: © Ron Sachs/CNP/Corbis; page 44: © Szenes
Jason/Corbis Sygma; page 45: © Reuters/Corbis; page 46: © Bettmann/Corbis; page 47: © Reuters/Corbis.

Library of Congress Control Number: 2007020029

ISBN 978-0-448-44787-2   10 9 8 7 6 5 4 3 2

HILLARY CLINTON
An American Journey

By Laura Driscoll
Illustrated by Judith V. Wood
and with photographs

Grosset & Dunlap

A Chilly Introduction

Washington, D.C.

January 20, 1993

It was a bitterly cold winter day. Even so, hundreds of thousands of people crowded outside the Capitol building. Some had been there for hours, bundled up in coats and hats. What kept them outside on such a cold day? They were waiting to see history being made.

As noontime drew near, all eyes looked toward the West Front of the Capitol. That's where William Jefferson Clinton stood.

Beside him was a woman in a dark blue coat and hat. In her hands was a Bible. Bill Clinton placed his hand on it as he took the oath of office, saying the words that made him . . . the president of the United States! And the woman at his side, Hillary Rodham Clinton, was now the first lady.

A powerful, well-known lawyer, Hillary had been an important part of Bill's campaign. She helped write speeches. She talked to reporters about Bill's ideas for the country. And she let people know that she had ideas, too—ideas about how to fix the United States' problems. Sometimes Bill joked that voters would get two presidents for the price of one.

But some Americans had strong ideas about what a first lady should be—and shouldn't be. They worried that Hillary wanted to run the country from behind the scenes. Others liked the fact that Hillary spoke her mind.

Like it or not, now she *was* the first lady. On the Capitol steps, the band played "Hail to the Chief," the presidential song. For eight years, from 1993 to 2001, Hillary heard that song played for her husband.

Now, "Hail to the Chief" might play for Hillary Rodham Clinton someday. She once described politics as "the art of making what appears to be impossible, possible." In the United States there has never been a woman president.

Will she be the first?

Growing Up, Speaking Up

Hillary Diane Rodham was born on October 26, 1947. She was the first child of Dorothy and Hugh Rodham. They lived in Park Ridge, Illinois, a suburb of Chicago.

Hillary's father was a successful businessman. The Rodhams had an expensive car and a nice house.

But Hillary and her two little brothers were not spoiled. They earned spending money by raking leaves, shoveling snow, and cutting the grass. One time, they had a weed-pulling contest. They got a penny for each dandelion.

Sometimes the family drove into downtown Chicago. They went to baseball games at Wrigley Field. On their way there, Hillary's parents took the long way through Chicago's poorest neighborhoods. They wanted their kids to

know how lucky they were. Hillary could see that some people had very little.

Hillary's mom cared for the children. She was a mother who liked having fun. On snowy days, she pulled the kids to the grocery store on a sled.

Her mother also made Hillary feel there was nothing she couldn't do. She taught Hillary to stand up for herself.

At school, Hillary always got good grades. Teachers left her in charge when they had to leave the room. Around the neighborhood, she organized kids in games. Even rowdy boys listened when Hillary spoke.

Hillary spoke her mind at home, too. Her dad had strong ideas about politics— how the government should work. At the dinner table there were lively debates— polite arguments about things like who should be president. Hillary was encouraged to have strong opinions and to back them up.

In high school, Hillary ran for student council president. She was the only girl running, and she lost.

After the election, one of the boys came up to her. "You're really stupid if you think a girl could be president," he said.

Hillary remembered those words for a long, long time.

Hillary in high school

A World Away from Home

In 1965, Hillary Rodham left home to start college at Wellesley, an all-women's school near Boston, Massachusetts. It was a big change from Park Ridge, Illinois. Hillary met girls who had traveled all over the world and who spoke foreign languages.

Hillary was used to being a top student. At Wellesley, the classes were much harder. At first she didn't think she was smart enough to be there. Still, she tried her best.

There was a lot going on in the world outside Wellesley. In the 1960s, many young Americans were against the war

the United States was fighting in North Vietnam. Others were angry about unfair treatment of black Americans.

Hillary took part in some protests against the government. At school, she wasn't shy about sharing her ideas. Hillary spoke. People listened.

Many of Hillary's ideas about the world were changing. She now believed that it was the government's job to help people in need. At Wellesley, she ran for student president—and won! Her classmates chose her to give a speech at graduation. It was the first time ever that a student had been chosen. What a great honor for Hillary!

In her speech, she talked about what needed to change in America and the importance of peaceful protests. She tried to give her class hope for the country's future.

Part of her speech was printed in *Life* magazine. People all over the country read it. Hillary was twenty-one. She had voiced what many young Americans were feeling.

21

After college, Hillary attended Yale Law School, a top school in the country.

One day in the library, Hillary met a fellow student. He was a tall young man from Arkansas with a beard and a mop of curly hair. His name was William Jefferson Clinton, but everyone called him Bill.

Hillary and Bill started to date. Like Hillary, Bill was very interested in politics. Like her, he was a Democrat. And like her, he was studying to be a lawyer.

Bill had big plans for his future. Already he had decided that one day he would be the governor of Arkansas.

First Lady of Arkansas

Seven years later, thirty-two-year-old
Bill Clinton was sworn in as the governor
of Arkansas. He was the youngest in the
state's history. Guess who was standing
next to him as he took the oath of office?
His wife, Hillary Rodham.

As a lawyer, Hillary had done important work of her own. In the early 1970s, she was part of the team investigating President Richard Nixon. (He resigned from the presidency in August of 1974.)

Hillary during the Nixon scandal

Hillary taught at a law school and then became a partner at a big law firm in Little Rock, Arkansas. She had made a name for herself: Hillary Rodham.

Now her husband was governor, but she still wanted to keep the last name she was born with.

Some people didn't like that. Why hadn't she taken her husband's last name? They didn't like the way she looked, either, with her unstyled hair and casual clothes. To them, she didn't *look* like a governor's wife.

Hillary tried not to listen to her critics. There were so many more important things—especially the birth of their daughter, Chelsea, in 1980. No, Hillary was too busy to worry about her hairdo.

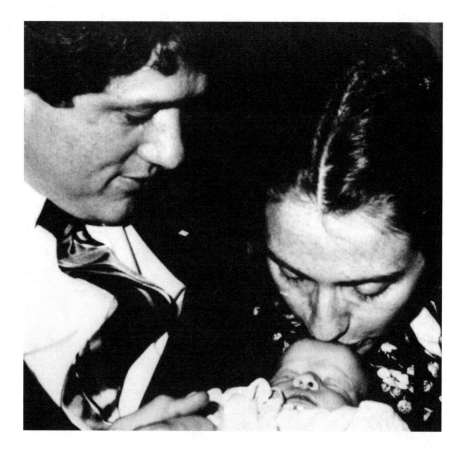

But in 1980, Bill Clinton did not win
a second term as governor. And Hillary
wanted to do everything she could to help
him win it back in 1982.

So during that campaign, Hillary started to look like the kind of first lady people were used to. She got a new hairstyle and more stylish clothes. She now called herself Hillary Rodham Clinton. Did any of this make a difference in the election? That is hard to say for sure, but Bill Clinton did win in 1982— and again in 1984, 1986, and 1988.

   As First Lady of Arkansas, Hillary
worked hard to improve schools. And she
still worked as a lawyer and took care of
Chelsea.

   It certainly was a busy life!

Then, in 1991, Hillary Rodham Clinton's life became even busier. Bill Clinton wanted to run for president in 1992. Hillary and Chelsea thought he could win.

And they were right. Their next home was the White House.

The White House Years

When Bill Clinton took office in 1993, the Clintons were tired from the long, hard campaign. But they were also very excited.

One of Bill Clinton's campaign promises was to provide better health care for poor Americans. He put Hillary in charge of the project. Why? Because he thought she was the best person for the job.

Critics of the Clintons didn't like it. Not one bit.

Hillary worked hard for health-care reform, or change. She was head of a team that made a list of changes. She presented them to Congress. At first, both Democrats and Republicans seemed to like her ideas. But the plan went nowhere. It never even came to a vote in Congress. It was a terrible defeat for Hillary Rodham Clinton.

There were other very difficult times for the First Lady. Worst of all was the scandal over her husband's romance with a young woman who worked at the White House. That cast a dark shadow over the family and over the end of Bill Clinton's presidency.

Despite this, Bill Clinton remained a popular president. And as the Clintons prepared to leave the White House, attention shifted to Hillary. Many people admired her for staying with her husband. Now people were encouraging *her* to run for elected office. Daniel Patrick Moynihan, a famous U.S. senator from New York, was retiring. Some Democrats thought Hillary could win his seat in the next senate election.

Hillary wasn't sure. But as a senator, she could help New Yorkers and all Americans. It was a chance she couldn't pass up.

So, while still first lady, she threw herself into her first political campaign. The Clintons bought a house in New York. She traveled all over the state—a big state with many different areas that had many different needs.

Daniel Patrick Moynihan and Hillary

Hillary talked to city dwellers and to rural farmers. Hillary got to know the voters and what they cared about. She was not from New York, and some people resented that. But she promised to fight for all New Yorkers.

Senator Clinton . . . for President?

On January 3, 2001, Hillary Rodham
Clinton was sworn in as a United
States senator. She beat a little-known
Republican congressman by a large
number of votes.

Before 1932, there had never been a
woman elected to the U.S. Senate.

In 2001, out of one hundred senators (two from each state), only thirteen were women. Hillary was the first wife of a president to hold an elected office.

On September 11, 2001, Senator Clinton had been in office for only eight months. That morning, the nation was rocked by terrorist attacks on New York City and Washington, D.C.

In New York City, three thousand people lost their lives when the Twin Towers fell. Nothing like this had ever happened in America. It was such a painful time. But besides the sadness, millions of dollars were needed to help the city recover and rebuild. Along with others, Senator Clinton worked to get the money from Washington, D.C., and help New Yorkers through a very difficult time.

In the Senate, Hillary, a Democrat, proved she could work well with Republicans. She helped pass laws to get better health care for people. She was a member of powerful committees.

By 2006, Hillary was no longer a newcomer to the people of New York. She ran for reelection and won by a mile.

Many people began to wonder if Senator Clinton would run for president in 2008. She knew that the road to the White House was long and hard. No woman had ever been the candidate of a major party.

Many had tried. In 1964, Senator Margaret Chase Smith of Maine hoped to be the Republicans' choice for president.

In 1972, an African-American congress-woman from New York, Shirley Chisholm, tried to win the Democratic nomination.

And in 1999, Elizabeth Dole, now a popular senator from North Carolina, campaigned to be the Republican nominee. None of these women got to be a candidate for president.

Some political experts say Hillary can't win. They say there are too many voters across the country who don't like her.

But others, like her mother, had taught Hillary there was nothing she couldn't do.

And so, on January 20, 2007—exactly two years before Inauguration Day 2009—Hillary Rodham Clinton announced she would give it a shot.

"I'm in," she announced. "And I'm in to win!"

Can she do it?

Only time—and the voters—will tell.